For Joey, my City of Angels baby.
Always shoot for the stars!
- J.F.M.

For my Mum and Dad.
- D.R.

LCCN 2019900123
ISBN 9781943147632

Text copyright © 2019 by Julia Finley Mosca
Illustrations by Daniel Rieley
Illustrations copyright © 2019 by The Innovation Press

Published by The Innovation Press
1001 4th Avenue, Suite 3200, Seattle, WA 98154
www.theinnovationpress.com

Printed and bound by Worzalla
Production Date June 2019
Plant Location: Stevens Point, Wisconsin

Cover lettering by Nicole LaRue
Cover art by Daniel Rieley
Book layout by Rose Clemens

WRITTEN BY
JULIA FINLEY MOSCA

ILLUSTRATED BY
DANIEL RIELEY

THE ASTRONAUT
WITH A SONG
FOR THE STARS
The Story Of Dr. Ellen Ochoa

If you have a MISSION,
a dream to explore,

but no one like you
has achieved it before,

listen up to this tale
of one STAR ENGINEER:

DR. ELLEN OCHOA,
a space pioneer!

In a city—Los Angeles
—one fateful day,

a baby was born
in the spring month of May.

This ELLEN, you'll find,
was no regular girl.

Yes, her future was BRIGHT,
even out of this world.

A grandchild of IMMIGRANTS,
Ellen was tough.

All her MEXICAN relatives . . .
they'd had it rough.

Her father would tell her,
"When I was in school,

people thought that LATINOS
would dirty the pool . . .

We could swim in the water,
but nice as that seemed,

we were *only* allowed
right before it was cleaned."

That RACISM hurt.
It was hateful and wrong.

And it taught him his children
would need to be STRONG.

RULES

Her mother agreed,
and she made it quite clear:

"If you want to SUCCEED,
don't stop LEARNING, my dear."

That was easy for Ellen—
so smart and astute.

And the thing she loved most?
Playing classical FLUTE.

FLUTE MUSIC

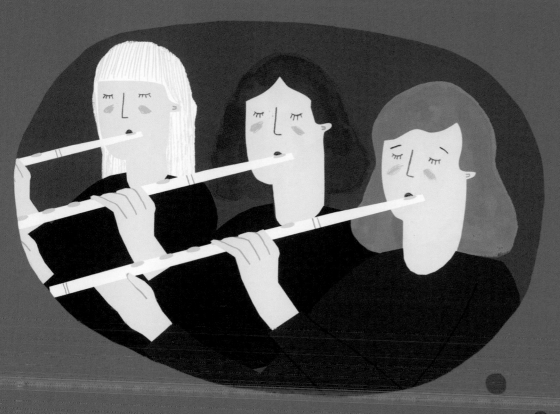

"I'll be a MUSICIAN,"
she thought, as she grew.

"An orchestra flutist . . .
Hey, that's what I'll do!"

Then in college she started
to think about SPACE . . .

but spacemen were men
(mostly white, was the case).

Unfair as that was,
Ellen made up her mind.

"I can study the shuttles,
and how they're designed."

"That's called ENGINEERING,"
her teacher explained.

"Forget it! That field is for boys,"
he proclaimed.

ENGINEERING

Well, never you fear.
Ellen got that degree.

And she saw SALLY RIDE
go to space on TV.

The first ASTRONAUT WOMAN!
And that's when she knew . . .

"If Sally can do it,
then I'll do it too!"

Alas, as you know,
life can sometimes be tricky.

The path to that dream?
Let's just say it got sticky.

She tried out for space school,
and what came of that?

The elite NASA Program
rejected her flat!

Did she stick with her goal?
Oh, you bet! She had BRAINS.

She learned more about ROCKETS
and PILOTING planes.

She INVENTED three systems,
which used beams of LIGHT—

helped computers to "see" things
that eyes couldn't quite.

And BOOM! It was time.
NASA finally took notice.

"You're IN!" they declared.
"We admire your FOCUS."

The training was hard—
no rest or recovery.

At last, it paid off.
Ellen boarded DISCOVERY!

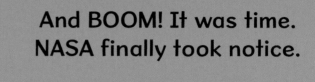

Ten,

Nine,

Eight . . .

The countdown began.
She held on with her might.

Then the girl from the City
of Angels took FLIGHT!

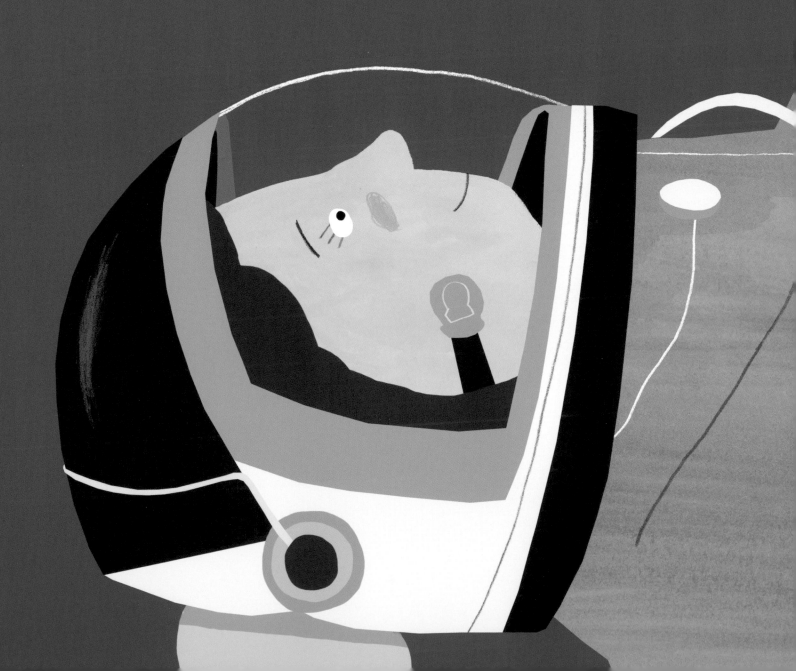

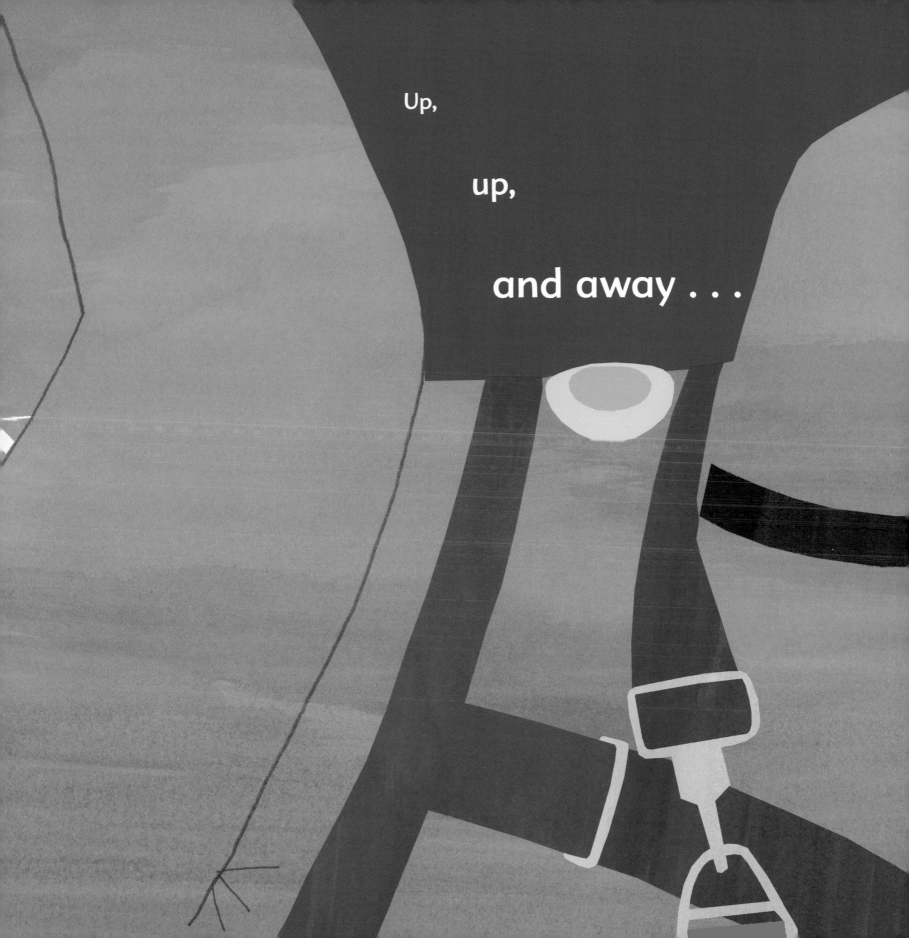

Up,

up,

and away . . .

. . . and up higher they flew.

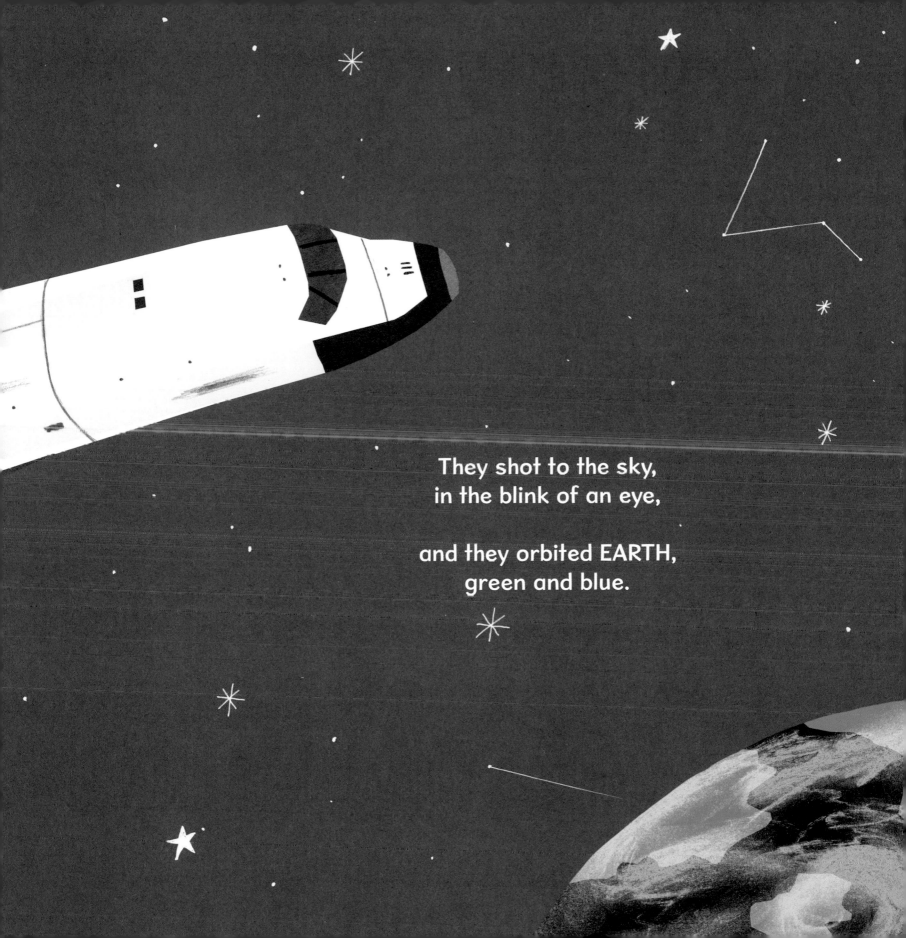

They shot to the sky,
in the blink of an eye,

and they orbited EARTH,
green and blue.

Now, guess what she did,
up so far, far away?

Ellen took out a FLUTE,
and she started to play.

But in space, people FLOAT,
so she strapped down her feet

(or she'd go for a loop
with each tweedle-dee-tweet!).

When she finished her tune,
she considered existence—

our planet, so tiny,
from such a great distance.

Though very few humans
had been in this place . . .

she'd done it:
THE WORLD'S FIRST LATINA IN SPACE!

If you're thinking THAT'S AWESOME,
you're right. It was sweet.

All those years of hard work
helped her conquer this feat.

And because of her skills,
NASA needed her more.

One mission is STELLAR,
but Ellen did FOUR!

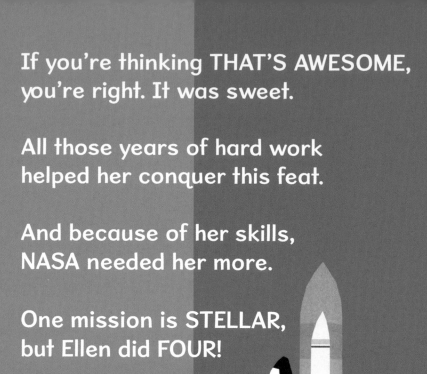

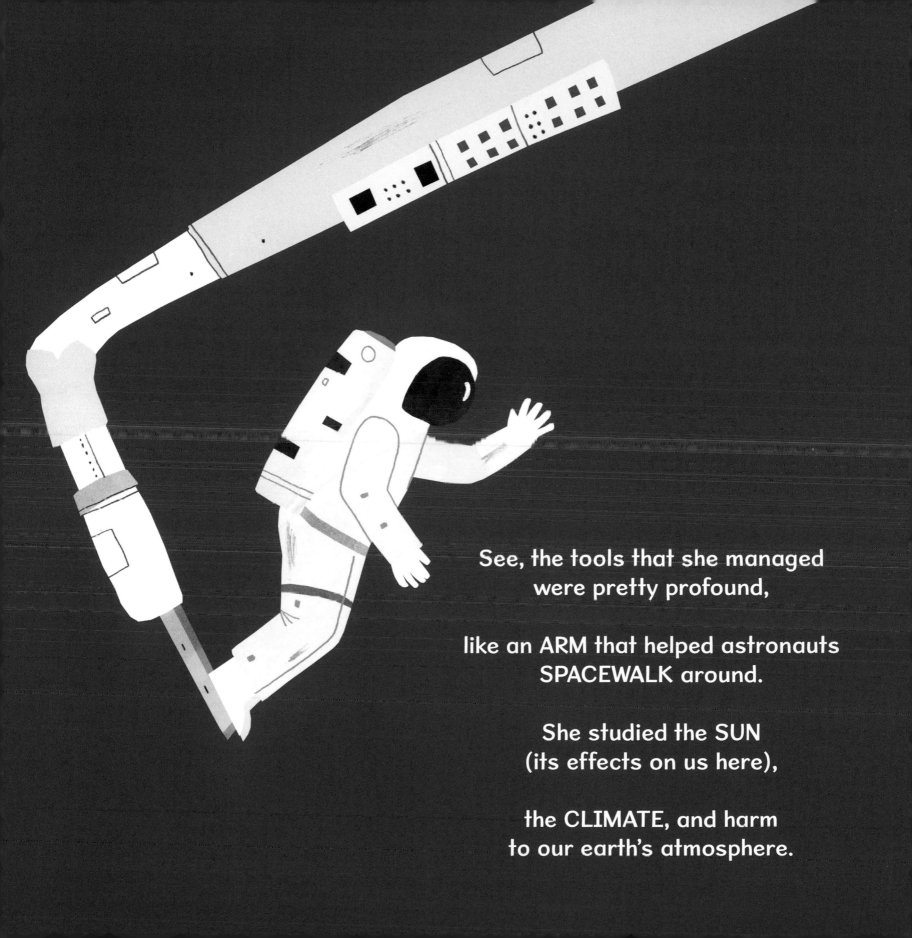

See, the tools that she managed
were pretty profound,

like an ARM that helped astronauts
SPACEWALK around.

She studied the SUN
(its effects on us here),

the CLIMATE, and harm
to our earth's atmosphere.

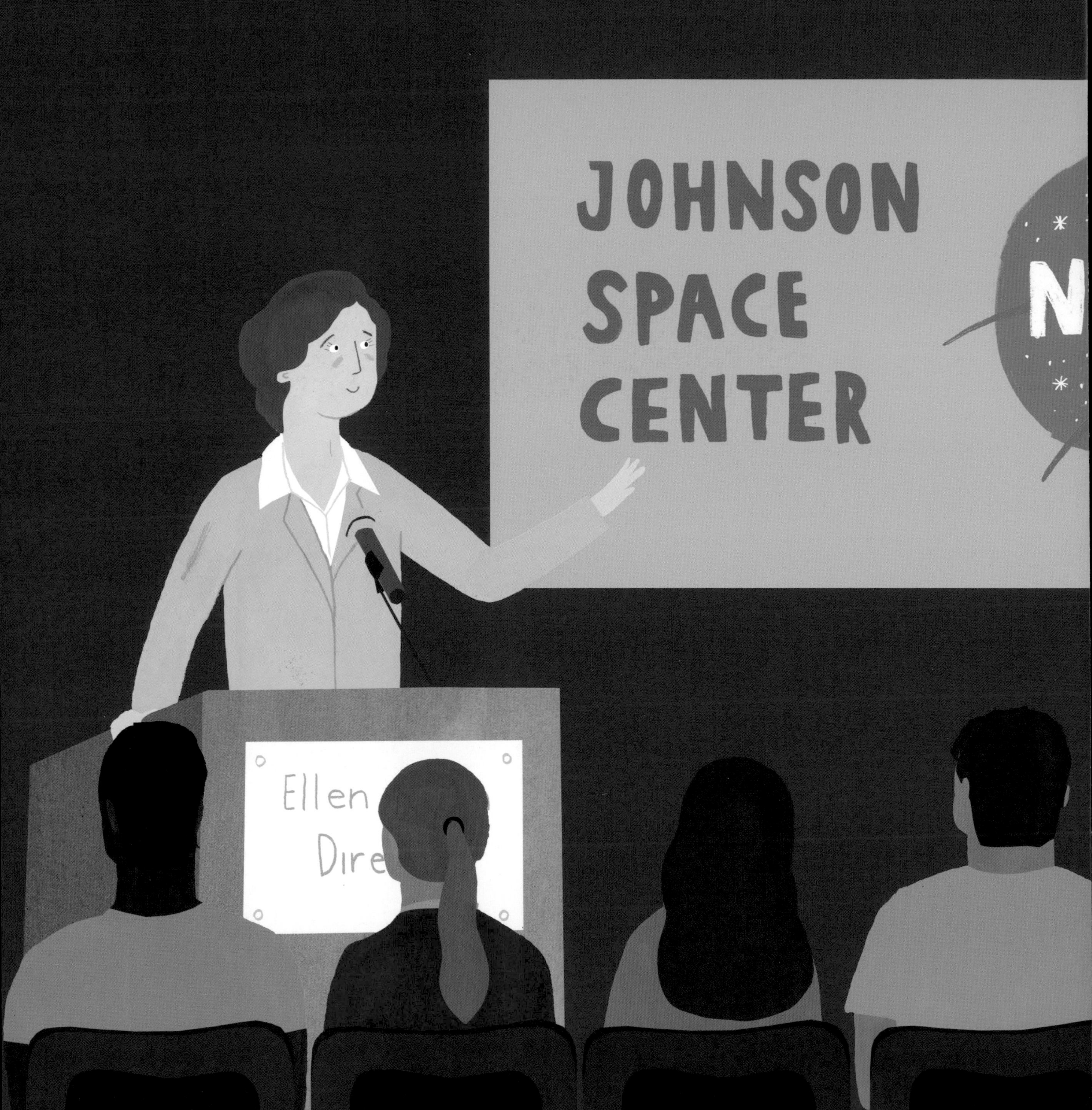
JOHNSON
SPACE
CENTER
Ellen
Dire

This research, of course,
brought her so much respect

that the JOHNSON SPACE CENTER
said, "Ellen, DIRECT!"

She accepted, and set
one more record, to boot . . .

**FIRST DIRECTOR
WITH LATIN AMERICAN ROOTS!**

Today, here on earth,
Ellen has a *new* mission—

to bring all of NASA's
great deeds recognition.

She still plays the flute,
and one note she'll impart:

"There's a place in this world
for both SCIENCE *and* ART."

Ellen Ochoa STEM Academy at Ben

Yes, all of this WISDOM and TALENT
(not small)

has won her AWARDS,
but one tribute beats all . . .

There are SCHOOLS with her name—
the best honor, indeed.

Since a good EDUCATION
helped Ellen succeed.

So, if life knocks you down,
lift your eyes to the sky.

Just dust off your wings.
Get back up. You can FLY!

With PERSISTENCE and KNOWLEDGE,
you'll surely go far.

Keep your head up, like Ellen,
and SHOOT FOR THE STARS!

Dear Readers,

Always persevere and take things one step at a time. Sometimes it can be daunting to think about going after a big goal, but if you break it down step by step, you'll often find it's a lot more doable.

Dr. Ellen Ochoa

FACTS AND TIDBITS FROM THE AUTHOR'S CHAT WITH DR. OCHOA

Launching a Love of Learning

When it came to her role models as a child, "the person that had the biggest impact on me was my mother," Dr. Ochoa told the author. "She was someone who was very interested in learning all kinds of things, and I think she passed on her enthusiasm for that to all of my brothers and sisters and me." Even though her mother didn't have a chance to go to college when she was young, that didn't stop the busy mom from making up for lost time. "After she was older and raising five kids, she took one college class a semester for many years . . . so, I think we all took inspiration from her," Dr. Ochoa explained. "Finally after about twenty years, she ended up graduating from college two years after I did!"

Shooting for Success

Growing up in a diverse family, Dr. Ochoa often heard her Mexican relatives speak of discrimination they endured as immigrants in the United States. "I remember being really taken aback," she said of the realization that they had been targeted for their race. Although she doesn't recall facing any racism herself, she said their stories definitely had an impact on her goals for the future. "I wanted to work hard and see what I could achieve, and hopefully be judged only for the work that I did."

Exploring a Galaxy of Options

While some kids know exactly what they want to be when they grow up, that wasn't the case for Dr. Ochoa, who always had many different interests. "I started playing the flute when I was ten. I also read a lot as a kid, and I liked math," she said. Even when she got older, the high school valedictorian wasn't quite sure what to study. "When I first went to college, I was thinking of either music or business, and then I tried a couple of other things. So, I really didn't have a good idea." Eventually, she said, "I came to the realization that math is a tool, and often used in other subjects. So, I started to explore a bit about what those other subjects were." From that point on, she focused on science, but it would still be a few more years before the idea of becoming an astronaut seemed possible.

Eclipsing All the Stereotypes

Choosing to pursue a future in STEM was a natural fit for Dr. Ochoa, but it wasn't always easy. She remembers meeting one professor who didn't take her seriously. "He was clearly trying to discourage me [from studying engineering]. He had different pieces of equipment on his desk, and he kept picking them up and saying, 'Well, you'd have to work with one of these. Does this REALLY interest you?'" Due to this experience, she wound up getting her first degree in physics instead. "What I mainly noticed was low expectations—a lot of people didn't expect women to excel. I think it's definitely changing, but you'll still find that," she said. Though she was quick to add, "I did have advisers in graduate school and in earlier jobs who supported me, and in general, they were all men. It's always about looking around to find those people who WILL support you, because they're out there." Even though Dr. Ochoa thinks women and minorities are still underrepresented in the field, "You absolutely see more women in STEM than when I first joined, and you see them in higher positions."

Orbiting With a New Perspective

Throughout her own high-powered career, Dr. Ochoa was able to see the world in a way most of us can only imagine—from outer space! "It's as fun as it seems! Just looking down at Earth and how really beautiful it is," she told the author. And just as you might expect, "Floating is really cool! But it can also make it difficult to do certain tasks," she explained. "You have to be very organized, very methodical, and figure out how to work in that different environment." For example, Dr. Ochoa learned that in order to play her flute without bumping into equipment, she had to strap down her feet. Simply blowing on the instrument created enough force to propel her around the tiny shuttle!

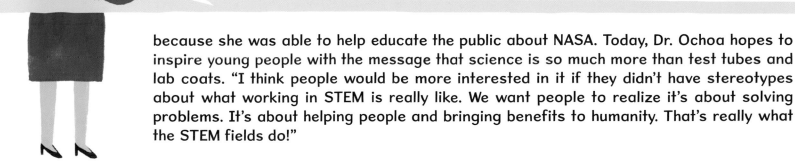

Landing Astronomical Honors

With all of these experiences and accomplishments under her belt, you might think that pinpointing her proudest moment would be hard for Dr. Ochoa. Yet, when asked about the highlight of her career, she didn't hesitate. "One of the neatest things is that I have six schools named after me!" she said. "With the importance of education to my mom—and what it did for my own career—that's kind of the highest honor you can get." She also believes that her most rewarding work was directing at the Johnson Space Center

because she was able to help educate the public about NASA. Today, Dr. Ochoa hopes to inspire young people with the message that science is so much more than test tubes and lab coats. "I think people would be more interested in it if they didn't have stereotypes about what working in STEM is really like. We want people to realize it's about solving problems. It's about helping people and bringing benefits to humanity. That's really what the STEM fields do!"

1958
Born on May 10, 1958, in Los Angeles, California

1980
Graduates as valedictorian from San Diego State University with physics degree

1981
Receives master's degree in electrical engineering from Stanford University

1984-1988
Co-invents three optical systems

1991
Officially completes intensive astronaut training

1993
Boards Discovery to become the first Latina astronaut in space

1975
Graduates as valedictorian from Grossmont High School in La Mesa, California

1985
Receives doctorate in electrical engineering from Stanford University

1990
Selected by NASA's astronaut training program

1983
Inspired by American astronaut Sally Ride to explore a career with NASA

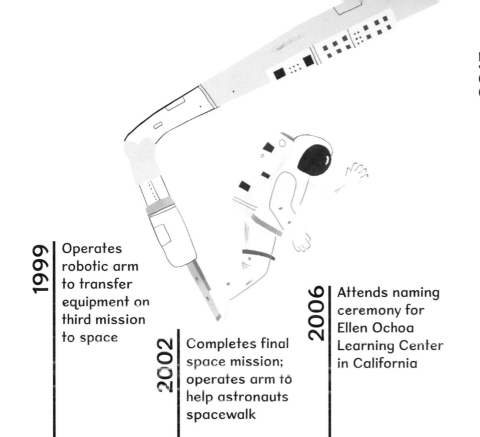

1999 Operates robotic arm to transfer equipment on third mission to space

2002 Completes final space mission; operates arm to help astronauts spacewalk

2006 Attends naming ceremony for Ellen Ochoa Learning Center in California

2015 Honored with National Space Grant Distinguished Service Award

2017 Inducted into the United States Astronaut Hall of Fame in Florida

2018 Retires from Johnson Space Center

1994 Flies aboard Atlantis to study the sun's effect on our atmosphere

2003 Receives NASA's highest award, the Distinguished Service Medal (and another in 2018)

2008 Named first woman Engineer of the Year by Hispanic committee HENAAC

2012 Appointed first Latina director of the Johnson Space Center in Houston

Present Resides in Idaho; continues to speak, mentor, and serve on many boards

Photo courtesy of NASA

Photo courtesy of NASA

ABOUT DR. OCHOA

Dr. Ellen Ochoa was born on May 10, 1958, in Los Angeles, California. From a very young age, it became clear that Ochoa had the smarts and skills to succeed at whatever she pursued. A multitalented scholar and musician, she explored many opportunities and bounced back from her fair share of setbacks before finally becoming a revered NASA superstar—the world's first Latina astronaut and first Latina director of the Johnson Space Center.

When Ochoa was just a year old, her parents, Joseph and Rosanne Ochoa, moved the family south to La Mesa, California. The renowned astronaut has long considered the San Diego community her hometown. Ochoa's Latin American heritage came to her through her father, whose family encountered both opportunity and discrimination after immigrating to the United States from Mexico. Tales of their experiences—like being told Latinos (or Hispanics) could only swim in the school swimming pool the day before it was to be cleaned—made Ochoa and her siblings even more determined to earn respect.

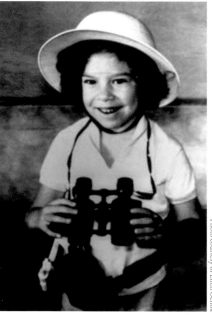

Photo courtesy of Ellen Ochoa

By the time Ochoa reached high school, her parents had divorced, leaving Rosanne to raise five children alone. The third of these five, Ochoa demonstrated a natural ability for music and played classical flute religiously. Her mother was always supportive of this interest (in fact, all five kids were involved in music), and she encouraged her children to study a wide variety of subjects. She believed a good education was the ticket to success and an interesting life. Ochoa had no difficulty fulfilling this request. She excelled in school, graduating as the valedictorian of her class at La Mesa's Grossmont High School in 1975.

Choosing to stay close to home, Ochoa attended college at San Diego State University. As a freshman in search of a major, she thought music seemed like an obvious fit. But after exploring other subjects like business, journalism, and computers, she considered a different path and ultimately decided on physics. This scientific field took full advantage of her fondness and aptitude for math. Not surprisingly, Ochoa graduated as valedictorian again in 1980 with a degree in physics. She then attended Stanford University, where she earned both a master's degree (1981) and a doctorate (1985) in electrical engineering, a field she had earlier been discouraged from pursuing as a woman.

During these years in graduate school, Ochoa performed research in the area of optics—the branch of physics that studies the behavior and properties of light. Some of the work she did made a lasting impact, like a process she helped develop that uses light technology to inspect objects (a computer circuit board, for example) and spot defects in a repeating pattern. The invention would go on to be patented in 1987. And somehow, between all of this innovation and study, Ochoa still found time to play her flute. She was a member of the established Stanford Symphony Orchestra, even earning the organization's Student Soloist Award. She also took notice of NASA while at Stanford, and was especially encouraged when the space program sent the first American woman, astronaut Sally Ride, to space in 1983.

In 1985, the newly graduated doctor applied for the astronaut program herself, but it would be almost two more years before she heard anything. Meanwhile, she began working at a government research facility called Sandia National Laboratories. In the spring of 1987, Ochoa learned she had made NASA's list of people to be interviewed. She traveled to the Johnson Space Center in Houston, Texas, where she underwent extensive tests and questioning. Unfortunately, she did not make the program that year.

Determined to try again, she focused on her work at the research center and helped develop two more optical inventions that would be patented in 1989 and 1990. One was for a device that uses light technology to locate a specific area or object, regardless of size or orientation. For example, it could help a spacecraft maneuver into a known landing site. The other patent was for a system that reduced noise in images. She also earned her private pilot's license. In 1988, Ochoa began a new job as chief of the

Intelligent Systems Technology Division at NASA's Ames Research Center, where she led a team of scientists who developed optical systems used specifically for space exploration.

Her work and leadership did not go unnoticed. In 1990, NASA selected Ochoa and twenty-two other candidates (from nearly two thousand applicants) to be part of their astronaut program. She reported for training that same year and made history as the world's first Latina astronaut, boarding the space shuttle Discovery in 1993.

During her time with NASA, Ochoa completed four space missions and logged over 978 hours in space. The focus of that first mission (April 8-17, 1993) was to better understand the effects of the sun and human activities on Earth's atmosphere. Ochoa's second mission, this time aboard the space shuttle Atlantis (November 3-14, 1994), continued that study. Her third trip to space (May 27-June 6, 1999) marked a return to Discovery, where crew members performed the first docking to the International Space Station. Ochoa used the Remote Manipulator System, a robotic arm, to deliver supplies in preparation for the first astronauts to live on the station. Her fourth and final mission (April 8-19, 2002, on Atlantis) returned to the International Space Station, where she operated a new station arm to maneuver spacewalkers around the space station. It was the first time this had been done.

In 2012, Ochoa began working for NASA in a whole new capacity. She became the director of the Johnson Space Center in Houston, Texas—setting yet another record as the first person of Latin American descent and second woman ever to hold the prestigious title. As director, Ochoa oversaw the entire astronaut program, mission operations for the International Space Station, and much more.

Throughout her long and impressive career, Ochoa has won many honors and awards. Her NASA awards include two Distinguished Service Medals (the organization's highest honor), the Exceptional Service Medal, the Outstanding Leadership Medal, and four Space Flight Medals. Other notable accolades include the Harvard Foundation Science Award, the Women in Aerospace Outstanding Achievement Award, the Hispanic Heritage Leadership Award, and the National Space Grant Distinguished Service Award. In 1995, she was named San Diego State University's Alumna of the Year, and in 2008, she was named Engineer of the Year by the Hispanic Engineer National Achievement Awards Corporation. She has been inducted into the California Hall of Fame and the acclaimed Astronaut Hall of Fame in Florida. Still, Ochoa says the greatest honor by far is having six schools named after her: Ellen Ochoa Middle School in Pasco, Washington; Ellen Ochoa Learning Center in Cudahy, California; Ellen Ochoa STEM Academy at Ben Milam Elementary in Grand Prairie, Texas; Ánimo Ellen Ochoa Charter Middle School in Los Angeles, California; Ellen Ochoa Prep Academy in Pico Rivera, California; and Ellen Ochoa Elementary School in Tulsa, Oklahoma.

In May 2018, at the age of sixty, Ochoa retired from the Johnson Space Center. Today, the scientist and mother of two sons lives in Idaho with her husband, Coe Fulmer Miles. She continues to use her voice and experience to educate the public about space. It is her hope that many more young people, especially women and minorities, will pursue and excel in the STEM fields. And, yes, she still finds time to play the flute!

As for the key to all of Ochoa's astronomical success, one thing is for sure: the renowned space pioneer refused to let negative people or low expectations get in the way of her dreams. If she had to try something more than once, or take a different path to reach her goals, she did it. It is this steadfast determination and positive outlook that makes Dr. Ellen Ochoa one of the most AMAZING SCIENTISTS and role models of our time.

Acknowledgements

The publisher, author, and illustrator are immensely grateful to Dr. Ellen Ochoa for speaking at length with the author, contributing personal photos, and providing helpful commentary throughout the creation of this book.

Bibliography

Articles

Hoekenga, Christine. "Ellen Ochoa: Science in Space." *Visionlearning* SCIRE-1, no. 7 (2014). https://www.visionlearning.com/en/library/Inside-Science/58/Ellen-Ochoa/201.

Brady, Hillary. "Making History Aboard *Discovery*." Smithsonian National Air and Space Museum website, April 15, 2018. https://airandspace.si.edu/stories/editorial/making-history-aboard-discovery.

McBride, Topanga. "Astronaut Ellen Ochoa: A love of science sent this pioneer to space." *Scholastic News*, Kid Press Corp, accessed May 1, 2019. http://www.scholastic.com/browse/article.jsp?id=3753806.

Books

Gibson, Karen Bush. *Women in Space: 23 Stories of First Flights, Scientific Missions, and Gravity-Breaking Adventures*. Chicago: Chicago Review Press, 2014. https://www.amazon.com/Women-Space-Scientific-Gravity-Breaking-Adventures/dp/1613748442.

Jackson, Libby. *Galaxy Girls: 50 Amazing Stories of Women in Space*. New York: Harper Design, 2018. https://www.amazon.com/Galaxy-Girls-Amazing-Stories-Women/dp/0062850210.

Videos/Television

"Women in Innovation: NASA's Dr. Ellen Ochoa," YouTube video, 4:47, posted by "USPTOvideo," April 23, 2018, https://www.youtube.com/watch?v=ZnMYy_wHk1s.

"Ellen Ochoa Astronaut," video interviews, Career Girls website, accessed May 1, 2019, https://www.careergirls.org/role-model/astronaut-0.

"Ellen Ochoa 2017 U.S. Astronaut Hall of Fame Inductee," YouTube video, 4:01, posted by Kennedy Space Center Visitor Complex, February 14, 2017, https://www.youtube.com/watch?v=qe9-ZEf__6k.

"Ellen Ochoa: Making History in Space," YouTube video, 20:38, posted by Goldman Sachs, October 11, 2018, https://www.youtube.com/watch?v=UHxt2moNPQ8.

Ready Jet Go! Season 2, episode 19, "Ellen Ochoa Visits the Treehouse." Aired March 18, 2019, on PBS. https://pbskids.org/video/ready-jet-go/3025281249.

Websites

National Aeronautics and Space Administration
(NASA) website. https://www.nasa.gov:

Space Center Houston website.
https://spacecenter.org.